How To Learn Programming

FM Bill Jordan

While every precaution has been taken in the preparation of this book, the publisher assumes no responsibility for errors or omissions, or for damages resulting from the use of the information contained herein.

Table of Contents

How To Learn Programming

Introduction

I would like to share my passion for programming so I have written a book about **programming**. This is not about any specific programming language, as there are principles that apply to any programming language. This is about every programming language.

This is not meant to be a programming reference book. It is more about general ideas.

An idea that is very specific can do a job very well. Unfortunately, something that is very specialised does not have a broad application.

The more abstract an idea is, the more situations it can be applied to, and the more useful the idea is.

The writing style will tend to be a *conversational* style. I write something like I would speak to you in person. Hopefully, this will make the text more fun to read.

The image on the front cover is a Mandelbrot, which is a type of computer generated image.

How and Why

When I was young, I read quite a few *How and Why* books. *How and Why* was a great series of children's books with lots of illustrations and questions and answers. There were How and Why books on many subjects. One was the *How and Why Book of Robots and Electronic Brains*. It was about computers.

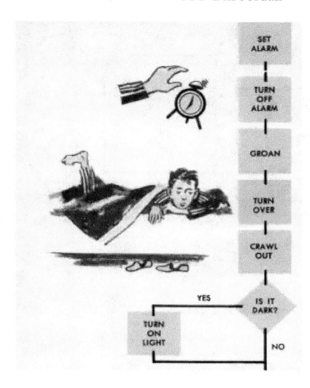

How To Learn Programming

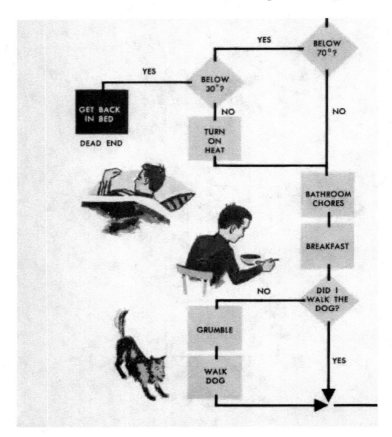

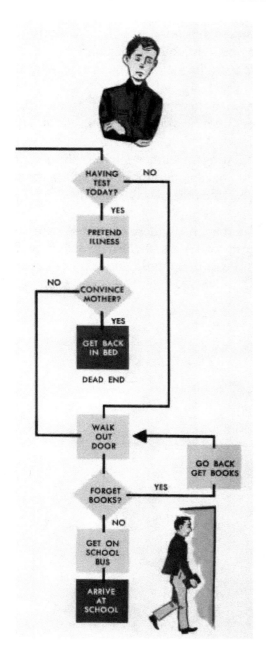

One section was on *Flow Charts*. A flow chart was a diagram demonstrating the flow of logic in a program.

How To Learn Programming

- Decisions were inside diamonds.
- Responses were inside light coloured squares.
- Ends of a sequence were inside dark squares.

The flow chart represented a humourous look at the decision making process of a student after he wakes up on a school day.

The book mentioned calculating machines such as the *abacus*. In those days, a highly skilled abacus operator could add faster than a computer. Computers have come a long way since.

The book also mentioned a machine called *The Turk*, which could beat all comers at the game of Chess. It turned out there was a midget hidden inside it who was making the moves.

FM Bill Jordan

MINITRAN

A programming language called MINITRAN had been created by
some of my secondary school maths teachers. It was based on the
FORTRAN language, the popular mathematical language of the
day. There were no home computers in those days, it was all mainframes.

We would write our programs on punch cards and hand them to
our teacher. A few days later, each student received a printout of
the program results. One day, my print-out consisted of two
hundred zeroes, causing some amusement to both the rest of the
class and me. Somewhere, there had been a division by zero error.

There were a few things I learned from using MINITRAN. While
programs used the arithmetic operators plus(+) and (-), they didn't
use times and divide. Instead, * was used for multiply. This made
sense as x could be confused with the letter x.

/ or \ was used for division (depending on the language). This
made sense, too, because the division symbol is not readily
accessible on a keyboard.

Another thing we were shown was the cryptic statement:

```
X = X + 1
```

This makes no sense in maths, but in programming, it means the
right-hand side of the equation is assigned to the left-hand side. In
other words, the new value of x becomes the old value of x plus
one, or one is added to x.

I did learn some basic concepts such as understanding that data
was information that a program used. There were punch cards
purely for data.

When I was 13, I was the second highest ranked junior chess

player in the state. Sometimes, I visited the Monash University chess club. I was told by a student that computer programming was just like seeing ahead moves in chess and that I should do it when I got older. This sowed the seed for an interest in programming.

At Careers Night at school, I learned that you get a job as a programmer by taking an aptitude test, which I was told I was good at.

When I was a teenager, I saw a movie called *2001:A Space Oddessy*, which featured HAL, a powerful computer. HAL could play Chess and pulled off a neat mate in four against its human opponent.

COBOL

I took a year off from university and did one subject at another tertiary institution. The subject was computer programming. I thought I would give programming a go.

One thing the teachers made clear from the outset was that computers could not think independently but could only do what they were programmed to do. They could not behave like HAL, who terminated the astronauts in hibernation unless they were programmed to do so.

In first term, we studied a machine language called PLAN. It was very easy. We were told we were taught it, so we would not want to code in machine language. Basically, everything was one step at a time.

The rest of the year we spent on COBOL which stood for Common Business Oriented Language. It was designed to be very similar to English. The assumption was that this would make it easier to program. Computer languages vary widely in how similar to English they are. For example, FORTRAN was a lot less like English than COBOL.

COBOL was a common language in the workplace. I remember a lecturer once saying that a COBOL programmer could earn $40 per hour, which was a very good rate. Upon hearing this, many students gasped in awe.

Shortly before the year 2000, COBOL programmers could make good money by fixing Y2K bugs in COBOL code.

Students were set assignments in which we had to design and create a program. I was irked by the fact that we were all designing the same program. I preferred the idea of creating a unique program.

How To Learn Programming

Programming was a slow process. First, the program had to be planned, preferably by creating flow charts.

The code had to be transcribed to a coding sheet, which consisted of a rectangular grid of rows and columns. Each square in the grid represented one character of code. Each line of program code was one line in the coding sheet.

The coding sheets were handed to the typing pool. A typist would type the characters on a machine that would generate punch cards. The program would be run on a mainframe. A printout would be handed to the student, usually about a week later.

Typists would frequently make errors. On one occasion, a typist left out a full stop. This resulted in my program having 50 errors. It was a long ride to the institution on my bicycle, and I didn't want to make the long trip more than weekly. I didn't do as many runs as I could have and didn't do so well. Anyway, the subject didn't count, so it was hard to take it seriously.

I do not remember much about COBOL and forgot about programming for more than 10 years. I vaguely remembered loops and what I mentioned here.

Home Computers

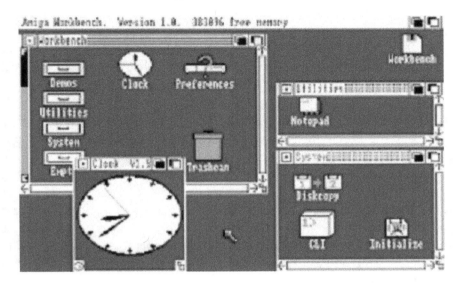

I had seen space invaders on a few home computers and had played *Apple Panic* and *Mystery house* on an Apple IIE in the early 80s. *Apple Panic* was a platform game in which you controlled a character that went up and down ladders and dug holes to knock apple monsters that were wandering around. When an apple was stuck in a hole, you could knock it through with a shovel.

Mystery House was one of the first graphics adventure games. The game starts with text saying that you have been invited to spend a weekend in a mysterious country house with 6 others. One by one, the guests are mysteriously murdered. The graphics were very simple. The characters looked like stick figures, and their eyes looked like crosses. Nonetheless, it was a pretty challenging game. The Apple had a **mouse**, which was something new for me.

A few decades later, I downloaded an Apple IIE emulator and solved Mystery House.

I had also played *Colossal Cave* on a mainframe at a computer

How To Learn Programming

exhibition. Colossal Cave was a classic text adventure, perhaps the first well-known one. The player could move in different directions, get, drop, and use items, and interact with characters in the game. There were no graphics at all. The entire game was text.

Different versions of the game and walk-throughs are now available on the net. I was surprised to learn that Colossal Cave was based on a real place.

A similar game I heard about was called *Hunt the Wumpus*. The playing area consisted of a series of connected rooms. You could move from room to room, but you were told when the Wumpus was nearby. You had to get him with an arrow before he got you.

I was at a friend's house in late 1988 and saw him playing a game called *Defender of the Crown* on a home PC. It was set in England at the time of Robin Hood. It had beautiful graphics, music, animation and interesting gameplay. I thought *I have got to get one of those.*

I asked friends about what type of home computer I should buy. Some said that I should get something that was IBM-compatible. My cousin, who was a self-employed programmer, told me over the phone about the best home computer on the market. I wrote down *Omega* and decided to get one, except that the name was actually *Amiga*, which apparently is Spanish for girlfriend.

The Amiga, unlike the IBM clones, had a monitor that was compatible with TVs. The Amiga could also use a TV, but this was not recommended. The Amiga had a mouse, like the Apple.

The Amiga was 5 years ahead of the other home computers. It had the best graphics, animation, and sound capabilities. It had a narrator device that sounded like Stephen Hawking. It's not great, but it's better than the other computers. It was a true multi-tasking computer, unlike present-day PCs, for example. It had many powerful machine code subroutines built into the ROM (Read Only Memory). It had a much simpler file system and built-in drivers for new hardware. It used 3.5-inch firm disks, unlike the 5.25-inch *floppy* disks that the PC used. The disks had 880 K of memory on them, which was a lot for the time. I was very happy with my choice.

AmigaBasic

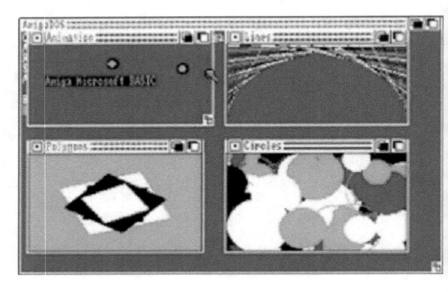

The evening I bought my Commodore Amiga 500, I looked at the two disks that came with it. The first was called *Workbench*, which was the start-up disk. The second was called *Extras* and had a number of utilities on it. I found it had a little picture with the name AmigaBasic on it. I later learned that these little pictures were called *icons*. Clicking on it ran the AmigaBasic program. In those days, many home computers came with a version of BASIC on them. This was a wise decision by computer developers as it encouraged many people to become interested in programming.

BASIC stands for **Beginners All purpose Symbolic Instruction Code**, though some people claimed none of these were true.

With some vague memories of MINITRAN and COBOL and armed with the AmigaBasic manual I wrote my very first real program. The AmigaBasic manual has been described as being as useful to a beginner as tits to a bull. One thing I found difficult was that code examples were frequently more complicated than necessary, often using many more keywords than the ones they were giving an example of.

That very first night, I wrote my very first program using only three commands: PRINT, GOTO, and STOP.

- PRINT displayed text on the screen. It had nothing to do with printing to a printer.
- GOTO caused the program to jump to a different line.
- STOP would cause the program to pause.

I used these commands to create a text adventure. The player was given several choices, and depending on his choice, he would branch to a different part of the story. When the program paused, you typed in GOTO, and one of the listed numbers, and the user would jump to that point in the game. A weakness of the program was that it needed to be run in *debug mode*. Debug mode helped the programmer to find and correct errors in the code.

A week or so later, a friend taught me how to use INPUT A$ correctly, so I was able to code the game properly.

```
INPUT A$
```

caused a program to pause until the user had typed something and pressed the Enter key.

New words

Entering the world of computers meant encountering many new words and concepts. I learned that:

- A *user* was the person running the program. In some contexts, the user was the programmer.
- An *icon* was a little picture that represented a program.
- A *menu* was a drop down list you could select from.
- *Execute* meant to run a program.
- Operating System is the program that runs the computer.
- *Code* was the text that a program was written in.
- RAM stood for Random Access Memory. It would be freed

when the computer was turned off.
- ROM stood for Read Only Memory. It was built into the hardware. The Amiga had many routines built into ROM.
- To *boot* a computer meant to start it up.
- An *application* was a program that did something useful.
- A utility was a program that helped you organise your computer.
- Multi media meant a program used sound, graphics, and animation.
- Games could be a lot of fun.
- And many more...

I also learned that computers could only understand machine code. At some point, the program code needs to be translated into machine code. AmigaBasic was an *interpreted* language, which meant it was translated into machine code instructions as it ran.

My cousin mailed me about 20 disks to get me started. They included games, utilities, and a paint program. After tiring myself from the games, I wanted to get into programming.

I only worked 2 days a week, so I had plenty of time to teach myself programming. Over the next 2 weeks, I worked hard on a program, and shortly afterwards, it was included in the vaunted Fred Fish public domain collection. The Fred Fish collection eventually had thousands of programs and was the most well-known Amiga PD collection.

Not long later, I was typing away on my keyboard on quite a hot day. It was so hot that my Amiga crashed. I lost several hours of work. After that, I learned the habit of saving my work regularly and saving it before I ran a program I had written.

AmigaBasic was a good language in many respects. It was better than versions of BASIC on other platforms. However, it had little support for the hardware. For example, there was no easy way to display an image on the screen. The Amiga was a very powerful graphics machine, so this was quite a shortcoming. This was a little unsurprising as AmigaBasic was written by Microsoft, which was a competing company. The future of the Amiga may have been very different if AmigaBasic had been better.

Pseudo Code

I learned that flow charts were not used as much as they used to be. If I used flow charts for some of my more complex projects, I would need thousands of pages.

Instead, pseudo code could be used. Pseudo code is a mixture of English and program code. It can initially be a rough draft and then later turned into real code.

The idea of statements was easy enough. A line of program code was a single statement, similar to a sentence in English.

AmigaBasic did not suffer from line numbers in the code. GW Basic on the PC had them. If you decided to insert more lines, you had a problem. Some programmers added line numbers in multiples of five so they could insert up to 4 lines between existing lines if needed. Programming with line numbers must have been a nightmare.

AmigaBasic did have line numbers, but as with most later languages, they were completely hidden from the user.

Editor

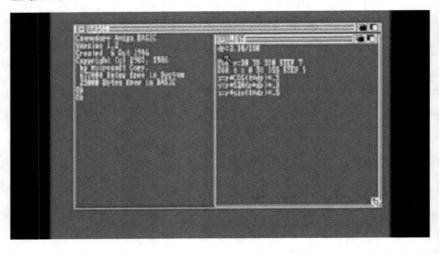

An AmigaBasic program had a single *source file*. This had a **.bas** extension (short for BASIC). Source files reflect the language in which the code is written. Regardless of the language, source files are plain text files. This makes editing program code simpler in some ways than editing other types of documents. Unlike, say, a **.docx** file, plain text files do store information about formatting, such as:

- Different fonts.
- Bold text.
- italic text.
- Underlined text.
- Different font sizes.
- etc.

This means that programming editors were (and are) a lot different from standard word processors. You never needed to format the text.

The AmigaBasic editor did not have many features. You could Cut, Copy, Paste, Find text, and not much else. Nor did you need to.

The AmigaBasic editor was *integrated*. This means the editor and the interpreter were both part of the same program. You could edit the program and run it from the menu. You could even do some editing while the program was running.

The AmigaBasic editor had some nice features. After you finished typing a line, it would tidy up the code for you.

- Spaces would be inserted between words.

- Closing double quotes would be added to string literals.

- All keywords and user-defined names would be converted to uppercase. (I have to admit I had not heard of uppercase and lowercase until I bought a computer.)

Program flow

Program flow was fairly intuitive. The idea of a program being a single text file was easy to understand.

The idea that a file consisted of a series of instructions that were performed (programming uses the unusual word **executed**) one after the other was also easy to understand.

It made sense that a *statement* was a single line of code.

It also made sense the natural flow would sometimes be altered.

Comparisons with English

There were quite a few similarities between English and BASIC.

For example:

- Statements were like sentences.
- The end of a line was like a full stop.
- Commands like PRINT were like verbs.
- Commands like SCREEN were like nouns.

- Variable names were like proper nouns.
- BASIC used prepositions like TO, AS, AND, OR etc.
- Double quotes around words were similar to quotes around spoken words.

There were also some major differences.

For example:

- Statements were sometimes a single word, shorter than what happens in English.
- The good news was that there were far fewer words in BASIC than in English, perhaps only 200.

Comments

Old style BASIC had the REM (short for remark) statement to indicate the rest of the line was a comment. A comment is text that doesn't get executed.

AmigaBasic had apostrophes as an alternative.

Comments could explain what the code was doing. You might write something clever, but 6 months down the track, you might forget what the code was doing.

Comments had another use. You could comment out and uncomment blocks of code. One use could be to test blocks of your code. This can be useful in **any** programming environment.

Operators

The AmigaBasic arithmetic operators were:

- + plus.
- - minus.
- * asterisk for multiply.
- / slash for divide.

This is the same as most programming languages. The first two were the same as their mathematical counterparts.

Using the asterisk instead of X made sense as it avoided confusion with the letter *X*.

Using the slash instead of the division sign made sense because the latter is not immediately visible on the keyboard.

Other symbols AmigaBasic used that were similar to maths were the comparison operators. These included:

- >

  Greater than.
- <

  Less than.
- >=

  Greater than or equal to.
- <=

  Less than or equal to.
- <>

  Not equal to.
- =

  Equal to.

Note that = was used for assignment as well. For example,

```
a = 1
```

assigns the value of 1 to the variable **a**.

There would be some advantages for conventional maths and computer maths to be more compatible. For example, maths textbooks could use asterisks for multiplication and slashes for division.

Variables

Variables were easy to understand because using them was similar to using algebra in maths at school.

The programmer invented names for variables, as they did for some other items, such as subroutines. There were rules for these *user-defined* names.

- They could use letters and numbers.
- They could not start with a number.
- They could not include spaces.
- They could not be too long.
- They could not be the same as a reserved word (a word in the language).
- A *string* variable ended in a $.

These rules were pretty similar in most languages.

Variables started with a default value, typically zero for number types and the empty string for *strings*.

Decisions

IF statements were very like the use of **If** in English.

For example,

If there is a good movie, then see the movie.

The main point is the question needs a true or false answer.

Something that evaluates to **true** or **false** is called *conditional*.

Adding ELSE was also like English. If it is raining then go inside else stay outside.

Programming languages generally have some kind of **if** statement.

Loops

It was easy to see that a program may repeat the same instructions over and over. For example, if you wanted to calculate the weekly pay for 1000 employees, you would want the same code to process each employee. You would I do not want the same code repeated 1000 times.

In AmigaBasic, there were two types of loops:

- FOR...NEXT
- WHILE...WEND

The FOR...The NEXT loop was good if you knew how many times you wanted to go through (traverse or iterate) the loop.

The first part of a loop might be:

```
FOR X = 1 TO 10
```

Loops used a variable that acted as a *loop counter*. It kept track of how many times you went through the loop.

In this case, X is the loop counter.

= sets it to a starting value.

The number after TO is the final value.

The counter increases by one each time through the loop.

```
FOR X = 1 TO 10
   PRINT X
NEXT
```

NEXT is the end of the loop. After reaching NEXT, the program jumps back to the FOR.

This loop prints out the numbers from 1 to 10.

You could have as many statements between the FOR and the NEXT as you liked.

Loops and Step

By default, the counter is incremented by one. STEP can be used to change this to any amount you like.

```
FOR X = 1 TO 10 STEP 2
    PRINT X
NEXT
```

Every second number is printed.

```
FOR X = 10 TO 1 STEP -1
    PRINT X
NEXT
```

In this case, STEP has a negative value. The starting value must be **more** than the final value, otherwise you will get an *infinite loop*.

STEP could use a variable.

```
FOR X = 1 TO 16 STEP X
    PRINT X
NEXT
```

Nested Loops

Placing a block of code inside another block of code is called *nesting*. Blocks could be nested to a *depth* of 2 or more.

Loops and Variables

Variables could be used instead of constant values.

```
FOR X = START TO FIN STEP INC
    PRINT X
NEXT
```

In this case, four different variables are used. Using variables makes code more flexible.

WHILE...WEND

The WHILE... WEND loop was good if you **did not know** how many times you wanted to go through the loop. It also uses a condition.

```
X = 1
WHILE x < 10
   X = X + 1
   PRINT X
NEXT
```

This loop prints out the numbers from 1 to 10, just like the previous FOR...NEXT loop. The statements

```
X = 1
```

gives the loop counter a starting value of 1.

Subroutines/functions

GOTO was easy enough to understand. You put a label in the code and GOTO would jump straight to the label.

GOSUB was somewhat similar. A GOSUB would take you straight to the start of a subroutine. So far, it was like GOTO. However, there was a return trip. At the end of the subroutine, the program would return automatically to the point immediately after where you came from.

This allowed you to use the same block of code from different points in the program. Unlike the GOTO label, in which there was a 1:1 relationship, the GOSUB subroutine had a many:1 relationship. Subroutines introduced the concept of reusing the same code.

In one program, I overdid the GOTOs. The code became so

convoluted it became very difficult to follow. I scrapped the program, which was a multiplayer space empires game, and restarted it from scratch.

I later read about *spaghetti code*, a term which very much fitted what I had created. A friend of mine who was a C programmer said that GOTOs were not needed at all. Having said that, there was another friend who said that there were rare cases in which a **goto** was the cleanest way to go.

AmigaBasic didn't have functions like more modern BASICs. Functions were similar to subroutines except that they sent back a value. The basic idea of a subroutine is present in pretty much all languages. There are different names for them, including subroutine, function, procedure, etc., but they are very similar.

Arrays

It took a little while to get my head around arrays, especially as the AmigaBasic manual did not explain them well.

An array is a bunch of similar variables, all with the same name but having a different number. A good analogy is a street address. Say there are 100 addresses in Main St. We could have an array called main with 100 elements. The first address is Main[1], while the last address is Main[100] etc. You could treat array elements as though they are ordinary variables.

Arrays had upper boundaries and lower boundaries. The upper boundary was the size of the array.

Arrays work very well with **FOR** loops. Arrays are fairly similar in every language.

Strings

How long is a piece of string?

A string can have no length at all. The zero-length string can be quite useful. In basic, it is represented by a double quote.

The maximum length depends on the language; in AmigaBasic, it's about 64,000 characters.

Strings can be multiple lines because they can include carriage returns.

ASCII Codes

ASCII stands for American standard character interchange. There are 256 ASCII characters, which happens to be the largest value that you can fit in an 8-bit byte.

There are printable characters, such as the digits 0-9, uppercase letters A-Z, lower case letters a-z (upper and lower case are different) and other characters such as

! @ # $ % ^ & * ( ) _ + , . / < > ? { } | [ ] \ _ + - =

etc.

There are also ASCII codes for non-printable characters such as Space, Enter, the four cursor keys, Tab, etc.

It was not necessary to memorise the entire table, but it was useful to have a copy for reference.

Screens

Amigas could be used with a monitor or a TV. Monitors were either NTSC, the US standard, or PAL, the European standard. The default resolution was 640 x 256 for PAL or 640 X 200 for NTSC.

When programs written for NTSC were run on a PAL system, there was a glitch in which the contents of the screen would become compressed, and there would be a blank region at the bottom. This was eventually fixed in a later version of the operating system. The resolution was high enough to create very good images.

Screen coordinates were 0,0 in the top left corner. The horizontal coordinate (usually x) would increase as you moved right, while the vertical coordinate (usually y) would increase as you moved down. Other computers used the same convention.

The Amiga had 4096 colours, which was sufficient for great graphics. I once saw an Amiga connected to a live video camera. It was just like watching TV.

Reading and Writing to Files

I learned that a file needed to be treated like a book. Before reading from it or writing to it, you needed to open it. When finished with it, you needed to close it.

Sequential files were the simplest. They were flat ASCII files or text files. That meant that the text within them had no formatting, such as different fonts and styles, such as bold and italic, etc. A good thing about ASCII files was that they could be edited with any text editor.

You could do a lot with them in AmigaBasic:

- Create a new file.
- Overwrite an existing file.
- Open a file for reading.
- Open a file for *appending*. This means that you could add to the end of a file.

There was no direct way to directly edit specific lines in the file. However, there were ways around this. One good way to use them was:

- Open the file for reading.
- Read the entire file, copying each line to an array element.
- Close the file.
- Change the array values within the program.
- Open the file for writing.
- Copy the array contents into the file.
- Close the file.

Sorting

I wanted to be able to add a high-score table to my programs. To do this, I needed the program to be able to read and write in a text file. This is a basic need of most programming languages. I also wanted to sort a list of numbers in order of size. I opened the file and stored the list of numbers in an array.

- The way I did this was to create a variable that stored the highest score and set it to zero.
- I would loop through the list, comparing the current best

score with the current value.
- If the current score were better, it would become the best score.
- I removed the best score from the list and remove it and repeat the process with the next item.
- The process could be repeated until all items have been sorted.

I later learned I had developed a **bubble sort**, which was one of about a dozen sorting algorithms I later came across. Over the years, more algorithms, including sorting algorithms, have been added to programming languages. It is suggested to see if an algorithm is already available before re-inventing the wheel.

In BASIC, I developed a lot of my own algorithms. One was for centering text on a screen. The basic idea was half the width of the screen. Subtract half the width of the text. The result would be the leftmost position of the text.

A useful one determined whether a number was odd or even. If there was no remainder after the number was divided by 2, then the number was even. Otherwise, the number was odd.

```
IF X MOD 2 = 0 THEN
```

You knew X was even. MOD was a function that returned the modulus (the remainder) of a division.

I used this to create a routine for displaying a chessboard. I used two nested FOR loops, one for the rows and the other for columns. This allowed me to draw 64 filled squares in rows and columns. If the total of the row and column was even, it was a dark square, else if it was odd, it was a light square. I later found a faster way by drawing one large light square for the entire board and then using the loops to draw the dark squares.

I drew the chess pieces by using graphics primitives. That is, lines, squares, rectangles, circles, and dots are used.

I want the program to know what square of the board they clicked on. I could find the x and y coordinates of the mouse. I subtracted the left and right offsets of the board and divided them by the width of the square. I could find which square they clicked on.

User Friendliness

A *user* is the person who uses a computer program. A user-friendly program:

- Does not suddenly stop the computer or behave badly, whatsoever the user may do. (The user is presumed to be a total idiot; this is not meant in an insulting way but to help the programmer take into account all possibilities, e.g., the user accidentally pressing two keys at once).
- Is as easy to use as possible.
- The computer should be waiting for you. You should not be waiting for the computer.
- There should be no point that the user thinks *What do I do now?*
- It is desirable the user can *undo* what they last did.
- It provides help and attempts to correct mistakes by the user.

The concept of *user-friendly* is very highly developed in programming, though several decades ago there were many *unfriendly* programs.

A Programming Example

My first non-trivial program was a ChessTutor program. I'
consisted of a series of chess puzzles for the user to solve. Within 2
weeks of buying my Amiga, I had a fully working version of the
program.

I hit a snag when the program reached 2000 lines of code. It had
reached a memory limit. This was largely due to the way I handled
program data. I had used DATA statements, which I found in a
library code. The data statements represented information that was
recorded on the data cards, which I was familiar with when using
MINITRAN and COBOL.

I asked my cousin about this and he said that the standard approach
was to store data in a separate file and access it from the program. I
had found this area daunting, though I persevered, and **file
handling** became a standard part of my programs. I also learned
the importance of separating program code and data.

I mailed a copy to my cousin (no Internet then) for testing. He told
me it had crashed. I had assumed that the user would always click
on the chessboard, as was the intent. He had clicked elsewhere on
the screen and caused a **division by zero error**. My attitude had
been if the user does not follow instructions, then it's bad luck if
the program crashes. I learned a valuable lesson. A program needs
to be **robust**, whatever the user does.

My cousin said I could make it *shareware*, which was a new
concept for me. The idea was users were invited to send a a small
sum of money, say $10, if they liked the program. I fixed the bug
and a short time later, a copy of it had been added to the Fred Fish
public domain collection. The Fred Fish was a very famous Amiga
public domain collection and had a lot of exposure. I waited for
money to come in, but none ever came, though I did get some later
with other shareware programs.

I wrote some more chess programs and sold a few dozen by asking for money upfront. In my chess programs, I needed to draw a chessboard on the screen.

AmigaBasic had the Line statement which could be used to draw coloured boxes.

The code was something like this.

```
For x = 1 to 8
 For y = 1 to 8 step 2
   line(20+x*40,20+y*40) - step(40,40),3,bf
 Next
Next
```

The basic chessboard was satisfactory, but the code was completely rigid.

- What if I wanted to move the chessboard somewhere else?
- What if I wanted to change the colours of the squares (or have an option
- where the user could change the colours)?
- What if I wanted to have the squares a different size?

The solution is to use variables instead of literal constants. Hard coded numeric and string values are very fixed.

```
line(dx+x*wd,dy+y*ht)-step(wd,ht),SquareColor,bf
```

dx and **dy** are offsets that affect the position of the top left-hand corner of the chessboard. The width and height of the squares are now variables (**wd** and **ht**), so they can be any size. (In fact, if they are of different values, then they don't even need to be squares.)

The square colour can be any colour I like.

By placing these variables as parameters in a function, I could have something like this:

```
DrawChessBoard(dx,dy,wd,ht,SquareColor)
```

I could then call this function at different times during the program and draw different types of chessboards.

The fewer literal constants there are in your program, the easier it will be to change your program.

I created some word games, including Hangman and Word Search. In Hangman, a player tries to guess the letters in a secret word. With every incorrect guess, a drawing of a man being hung is closer to completion. There are about 12 steps in total.

An algorithm for toggling a variable between two values might be:

```
x = 3 - x
```

If x is 1 it will become 2, if its 2 it will become one.

There were algorithms for randomly jumbling up words, creating a straight path on the screen, etc.

I enjoyed solving puzzles and was able to create algorithms without having to look up books.

Readability

I read about ways to make code more readable.

Meaningful Names

One way was to use meaningful *user-defined* names. User-defined in the context of programming really means programmer-defined. User-defined names were used for names of variables, constants, subroutines, labels, etc.

There were some rules for what names could be. Names could start with a letter but not a number. This seems to be standard across languages. Names could not include spaces or other non-alphanumeric characters.

It would have been better if the names were not too long.

Indentation

Wisely used indentation can make code easier to read. Rather than writing several nested loops like:

```
FOR X = TO 100
FOR Y = 1 TO 100
FOR Z = 1 TO 100
PRINT X + Y + Z
NEXT
NEXT
NEXT
```

You could write it like this:

```
FOR X = TO 100
    FOR Y = 1 TO 100
        FOR Z = 1 TO 100
            PRINT X + Y + Z
        NEXT
    NEXT
NEXT
```

This made it easier to see where the starts and ends of loops matched.

Rather than writing several nested decisions like:

```
IF X > 0 THEN
PRINT "x is greater than zero."A"
END IF
```

You could write it like this:

```
IF X > 0 THEN
    PRINT "x is greater than zero."A"
END IF
```

Rather than writing several nested decisions like:

```
IF X >0 THEN
```

```
IF Y > 0 THEN
IF Z > 0 THEN
PRINT "x,y and z are all greater than zero."A"
END IF
END IF
END IF
```

You could write it like this:

```
IF X >0 THEN
    IF Y > 0 THEN
        IF Z > 0 THEN
            PRINT "x,y and z are all greater than
zero."A"
        END IF
    END IF
END IF
```

These days, many code editors indent code automatically.

Comments

Comments could help describe what parts of the code are doing. A good point was made was that you might know what the code is doing, but will you remember 6 months down the track, especially if you have not looked at the code for a while.

Flexibility

A program is not a fixed thing. It is dynamic. Who can say that even when you have completed a program, and you think it's pretty good, there will not be any more features that you can add to it later?

The easier it is to change a program, the better. How can a program be made easy to change?

Design it so it only needs to be changed in one place.

Structure

Non-programmers sometimes presume that programming is an exact science. Actually, it is more like an art form. There are often different ways of achieving the same ends.

One of the most important ideas is structure. The more structured (organised) the design of a program is, the less likely it is for flaws to develop in it. It is also easier to check for their presence and remove them.

Structure is not always an impediment to creative ideas. Structure can actually assist creativity in many ways. Structures can be very useful, but too much structuring can be restrictive in certain contexts.

Design

In a program, design is very important. Some time spent in the design phase can save a lot of time later. Sometimes, ideas can be completely eliminated during the design phase.

Specific things can be worked out on paper, and a general overall feel can be developed.

Re-Usability

An important concept is re-usability. Sections of programs can be written in such a way that they can be plugged easily into new programs. Re-usability avoids the need for *reinventing the wheel.*

Maintenance

A similar concept is maintenance. An existing program may need small readjustments made to it from time to time. A well-designed and structured program is easier to maintain.

Divide And Conquer

This is the idea of breaking up a complex task into smaller, more manageable tasks. There is a story about a King who challenges a small boy to jump to the top of the King's castle. The small boy does it. Not in one giant step but by making a series of many small steps.

There are other computer concepts that could be applied to other areas. To some extent, there are ideas common to all or many areas of specialised activity, whether it's the study of molluscs or flying kites. In the computer environment, something has happened to me more often than in other environments.

After having done something, later you become aware there is a way in which you could have done it faster and/or better.

Upgrades

Many programs are constantly changing and being upgraded. They are continually being made more efficient, easier to use and so on. Sometimes, changes are implemented in response to users suggestions. This is a very dynamic approach, in contrast to many goods and items, which tend to be static.

Debugging

Apparently, the word *bug* arose from a time in which moths would get into early mainframes and cause damage. A program bug is an error in the code. Debugging is the art of removing errors in the code. Programmers may spend a lot of time attempting to find out why a program doesn't behave as it ought. This process is called debugging.

Try things in a different order. One order might work when another order does not.

Testing

Associated with debugging is the testing process. During testing, as many possible situations as practical are tested. Unlikely combinations of events are tested, as well as the more frequent ones.

I read that regardless of the language used, there were two types of errors:

- Syntax errors.
- Logic errors.

Syntax Errors

A syntax error happens when the rules of the language are not followed.

For example:

- A keyword is spelled incorrectly.
- Brackets are not matched up.
- A user-defined name uses incorrect characters.
- Symbols are misplaced or unrecognised.
- Spaces are not used when they need to be.

In an interpreted language like AmigaBasic, most syntax errors are caught on the fly while the program is running. Unfortunately, you never know when they will strike. Some syntax errors are caught before the program starts.

Logic Errors

A logic error isn't an error in the code as such. It's when the program doesn't do what it is intended. For example, if you wrote a function that was meant to give you the square of a number but gave you the square root, then you have a problem.

Syntax errors of inexperienced programs often result from the lack of familiarity with the language.

Many syntax errors are the result of typos. A comma or full stop missing, incorrectly spelled words, etc., could all result in errors.

Debug Mode

AmigaBasic could enter debug mode. AmigaBasic had some powerful debugging features.

You could **step** through the code, one line at a time.

Stepping through paused the program, during which time you could use the *immediate* window.

In this, you could type a statement and press Enter, and it would run immediately. A commonly used one was PRINT. This could be used to display the current value of a variable.

For example, ?x followed by Enter, would cause the statement to expand to

```
PRINT X
```

and running it could display the current value of X.

Division by Zero

As I learned in my early days of MINITRAN, computers tend to crash when dividing by zero. This bug can be removed by adding an IF statement to parts of the code in which this could happen.

For example:

```
IF X>0 THEN
    Z = Y/X
END IF
```

Note that it doesn't matter if Y is zero.

Infinite Loops

There are a variety of ways unintentional infinite loops could be created.

For example:

```
FOR X = 1 TO 100
   PRINT X
   X = X - 1
NEXT
```

X never gets to 100, so the loop never completes.

Crashing the computer

Fortunately, this did not happen often with AmigaBasic. It was too high a level language. This is the worst type of bug, as you have to reboot the computer, which is the most annoying thing for other users. It's especially annoying for the programmer if they have not saved their work before running the program.

Tricky debugging

While many logic bugs could be found quickly, some could be very elusive. There is a programmer's joke:

How To Learn Programming

How many programmers does it take to put in a light bulb?

Answer: One plus 99 to debug the house.

It has been seen that 90% of programming time is spent on 10% of the code.

Reading the code

Carefully reading through the code can find a lot of bugs. This can be quicker than methods such as stepping through the code.

Isolating the code

It's important to find what code is causing the logic error. Techniques of debugging include isolating the point in the program where the problem happens. There are several ways of isolating the cause. Disabling parts of the program is one way of achieving this.

Commenting out code.

This can be a way of turning off part of the code. If you comment out some code, test the program, and the bug has vanished, then you know that the bug has something to do with that code. If a large block of code has been commented out, then you can gradually remove the comments to help you find the exact location of the cause of the bug.

Print statements.

Placing **PRINT** statements at strategic points in the code could help to reveal errors. A programmer once said to me that you will find any bug eventually if you display the current values of all the variables as you run the program.

Compiled BASIC

HiSoft BASIC

*Fast, Interactive BASIC Compiler
for the Commodore Amiga*

AmigaBasic was an interpreted language. The interpreter program translates each line into machine code as it runs.

I learned that some languages, like C, use a compiler. The compiler was a program that converted the entire source code into machine code.

The source code was untouched, and a new **.exe** file was created. (The suffix **.exe** means the file is an executable program.)

All you needed to do to run the .exe file on another computer was to copy it across.

One advantage was speed. Also, all **syntax** errors were found before the program was run. In fact, it couldn't run if there were any syntax errors. Another was that some undetected errors could be found.

Another was that the source code was not distributed so that a user couldn't see it.

Interpreted languages had some advantages, though. You didn't have to build the program, and in some ways, they were easier to debug.

Basic compilers started appearing on the market. I bought one,

How To Learn Programming

which created a faster side.

Around this time, I mentored another self-taught programmer. He used Commodore Basic, which was a sight to see. There were line numbers. There were no spaces between the words to save memory. For example, a line of code could be:

```
55FORX=1TO10
```

The equivalent in AmigaBasic would be:

```
FOR X = 1 TO 10
```

He had done quite well selling educational programs in women's magazines and was a registered commodore developer. He wanted to switch to AmigaBasic.

I picked up some good tips from him. If you are selling a program to someone, it must look good; it must do what it's expected to and be bugless. He tested a few of my programs in one way by quickly pressing a whole lot of keys simultaneously.

Print out the source code and read it away from a computer. You will see things in different ways and come up with all sorts of ideas.

He had a shortcut for converting letters to numbers and vice versa by using CHR$ and ASC.

ASC was a function that would return the ASCII value of a character. For example,

```
ASC("A")
```

would return 65.

CHR$ was a function that would return a character that had the given ASCII value. For example,

```
CHR$(65)
```

would return "A". If x was a digit,

```
CHR$(x + 48)
```

would return the character that represented x.

I once came across a book he had written on programming in a second-hand bookshop. It included how to write a complete *Space Invaders* type game. It included the use of the low-level PEEK and POKE commands.

```
PEEK
```

allowed a program to read what was at a given memory address.

```
POKE
```

allowed a program to write a value at the given memory address. Using POKE was a risky practice because using it in error could crash the computer. Some years later, he took one of my Visual Basic courses.

Larger Programs

Within a year of programming, I created larger programs, some 5000+ lines. I mostly used variables with arithmetic and algebra, string manipulation, decisions with IF and ELSE, arrays and loops, subroutines and functions. I was reading keyboard and mouse input and outputting text, graphics and images to the screen. I could do a lot with a relatively small number of ideas. You do need to use everything in a language to program effectively.

I created dozens of games, utilities and educational programs written in compiled AmigaBasic. I released many of these into the public domain, mostly as shareware programs. Some of my programs were reviewed in glossy Amiga magazines like AmigaFormat.

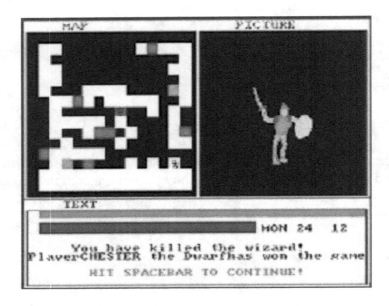

In 2016, I received an email enquiring whether I was the Bill Jordan who wrote the 1991 Amiga game *Dungeon of Nadroj*. This game had once won an award for PD game of the month by a UK public domain (PD) library. After I replied in the affirmative, the author of the email wrote a review of the game after all those years. Amazing.

Two sides to programming

What is a good program? There are two sides to a program:

- The outer side: this is what the user sees.
- The inner side: (the source code) This is invisible from the user but vital to programmers.

Although the outer is a manifestation of the inner, the two are worlds apart.

Programmers can get so lost in the inner world that they forget that the purpose of writing a program is to create a program.

Users don't know or care what your source code is like. They are only interested in the outer manifestation of the program. I once heard of a programmer who took a long time to develop a program and found something people didn't like his program because they didn't like its icon.

It's quite different coding for yourself from coding in a team. In a team, it's important for other people to understand or maintain your code. A programmer can leave a workplace, and it can be challenging for other programmers to take on where they have left off.

The Outer

- It needs to be user-friendly.
- Robust (a program that crashes frequently and is not user-friendly).
- Easy to use.
- Intuitive
- It should look good.

The Inner

It is desirable it is:

- Fast to develop.
- Easy to modify.
- Easy to debug.
- Easy to test.

Amiga User Group

After owning an Amiga for a few months, I decided to look for an Amiga user group. A friend of mine and I drove around looking for a user group that was holding a meeting in a community centre. We saw a group of men of all shapes and sizes, some bald, others with long hair and some bespectacled. My friend said that looks like a bunch of computer nerds, and he was right. I went to many of their weekly meetings over the next several years.

Meetings included hardware and software demonstrations. Software included games, utilities and applications. The group had an extensive public domain library, which included a subscription to the excellent MegaDisc magazine on disk. One meeting included a demonstration of an Amiga running an Amiga screen, an IBM and an Apple emulator **simultaneously**.

The Amiga did not come with a hard drive. At one meeting, a hard drive was demonstrated. The presenter said that after seeing a hard drive in action for a few moments, he decided to get one.

Bulletin Board

The Amiga User group had a BBS (Bulletin Board System), which had about 1000 users. I was a little reluctant to join it as I thought it would take time away from programming, which it did. It was like a mini-Internet. With my trusty 2400 baud modem (which was pretty fast for those days), I could download an 880k disk in only about 45 minutes. It was about 5% of the speed of my dial-up modem when I connected to the Internet about 5 years later.

You could exchange messages with people in a manner not unlike email.

There were a number of online games that you could play. They used a system in which a player could log into a game and play their turn. While a player was having their turn, no other players could log in. This would have made it much easier to program the games. This was similar to systems in which one user could access a database and edit it while any other users logging in were locked out, though they could still view data in read-only mode.

One game was *Global War*, which was an online version of the classic world conquest board game *Risk*. You had one turn a day against about five opponents.

There was a game called *Blackmar's Dungeon* , which was a Dungeons and Dragons role-playing game. Your character could explore the maze like dungeon while fighting monsters and finding treasure. The graphics in the game were composed of coloured ASCII characters. This was to speed up the transfer of data.

The Development Cycle

I met a guy called Greg who had developed an interesting idea for distributing software. The basic idea was that a demo version of a program would be placed in the public domain. If a user wanted to purchase the full version they could do so and activate the full version by receiving a set of magic numbers. Buyers were encouraged to give demo copies of the program to their friends. If their friends purchased a copy, the first person would receive a kickback, and they would get a percentage of the fee.

I had heard about *beta* versions of programs. These were programs that had been developed to the point that the developer was happy with them, and they were ready to be tested by other people.

What was new was the concept of an *alpha* version. This was the point at which the programmer had completed the program but not yet tested it himself. Greg had created a scale of 1-10, indicating how well a program had been tested. It was something like this:

- 1 It's OK.
- 2 Early Alpha
- 3 - It has been tested by the programmer a few times.
- 4-5 More rigorous testing by the programmer.

- 6-9 Various stages of beta testing.
- 10 Full beta testing cycle completed.

Having had a few people beta test some of my programs over the years, one thing I learned was it was best if testers make notes. Otherwise, you may get feedback like *There was something no user-friendly with the program. I just cannot remember what i was.*

Assembly

A big advantage of high-level languages is the faster development time. A big advantage of low-level languages is that you get exactly what you want. Somebody summed it up once by saying:

- With a high-level language, you are given the bucket.
- With assembly, you get exactly what kind of bucket you want.

Some Amiga games were written in assembly to make the best use of the hardware.

I came across a PD disk containing some assembly routines for AmigaBasic. They were brilliant and could do many of the things that you couldn't do directly in AmigaBasic, such as display images, change the text font, colour and size, etc. It was a dream come true. I had spent a lot of time attempting to do what AmigaBasic was not directly capable of.

Amos Basic

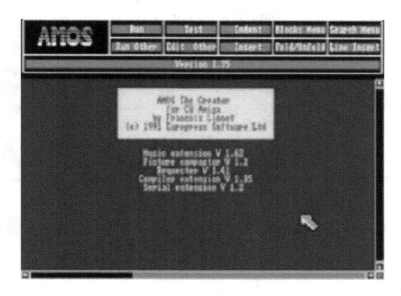

Amos Basic was a high-level language, similar to AmigaBasic in some ways, but included a lot of low-level functions, including ways to manipulate images and sprites, change the text font, colour and size, animate, play sounds, etc.

It could do many things I couldn't do in AmigaBasic. It looked impressive, so I used this instead of AmigaBasic with the new assembly routines.

It had a rather unusual interface as a result of being ported from the Atari St. It did not use the standard Amiga drop-down menus, which made it awkward to use. A version called Amos Professional was later released, which included the standard menus.

It was very popular and became the best-selling program on the Amiga. However, it had been released in a hurry. Bug patches were released. One patch fixed 15 bugs, 14 of which I had encountered.

One serious weakness of Amos was that the **start** of a variable name could not match any one of about 600 keywords (most of which were really library functions). For example, Forest could not be used because it started with For, Town could not be used because it started with To, etc.

I released a number of AMOS programs into the public domain. I had three programs sold as *licenceware* in the UK and Europe. I received several cheques for a few thousand pounds, which represented quite a few sales.

There were many excellent games and educational programs written in AMOS. A comment was made that a good educational program educated while entertaining.

AMOS was a stepping stone for many people who later moved to languages such as C++.

Blitz Basic

Blitz Basic was a program similar to Amos Basic, which a group of New Zealanders created. Like the early versions of Amos, it was a little buggy.

I created a game with Blitz Basic called Ethos. The theme was ancient Greek mythology. Your character could travel around the ancient world and have various adventures, such as meeting Greek Gods.

A few years later, a Blitz Basic 2, which was **much** better, was released. It was even bigger and better than the best versions of Amos. My cousin met one of the programmers, whom he described as a scruffy rebel.

Apple IIE

I was able to borrow an Apple IIE from a friend and convert one of my chess programs to the Apple. I learned a lot about the Apple IIE in the process. The Apple IIE was the computer I had played *Mystery House* on some years before. It was ancient compared with an Amiga. Using it was like stepping into the past with a time machine.

QuickBasic for DOS

Some people said I should *port* my chess programs to the IBM PC, so I met with a friend who had QuickBasic for DOS at his workplace. This was the first programming language I saw that had online help. It was pretty impressive. You could highlight a word, press F1 and help on that word was displayed.

Modern programming languages may have gigabytes of help files, usually on the net. One can get lost reading through It all was not knowing what was important and what wasn't, and it was not clear what had been read before.

There is a real danger that programmers sometimes cannot see the trees for the woods.

In some ways, it was simpler then; all the help was already on your computer.

QuickBasic was quite similar to AmigaBasic, which was not really surprising because they were both written by Microsoft. The IBM-compatible computer it was on was not nearly as powerful as an Amiga, though.

C language

I went to a short course on C language, which a member of the user group presented. The presenter showed us a *Hello World!* program, which I had not seen before. There was a convention that the first program someone would write in a new language was a *Hello World* program, which would do nothing more but display *Hello World* on the screen.

```
PRINT "Hello World!"A"
```

This is the *Hello World* program in BASIC.

```
#include

void main()
{
printf("Hello World!"A");
}
```

This is the *Hello World* program in C. The first thing noticeable is that the C code is longer. BASIC is a *high-level* language. There is a high ratio of machine code instructions to program code. C is a *middle level* language. There is sometimes a high ratio and sometimes a low ratio. C could sometimes be close to machine code and other times very high level.

Source file names ended in **.c**. Header file names ended in **.h**. A header file was a separate source file. The compiled program file name ended in **.exe**.

The first line in the C code is a directive. It had a similar effect to copying and pasting the code from the conio.h file into the source code. The angled brackets indicated that the header file was part of the standard library.

All C programs had a main function. This was the entry point to the program. The return type of main in this case was **void**. This means that no value was returned. The brackets after the word main was in all function definitions. In this case, they were empty, indicating that no arguments were passed to them. The curly brackets{} represented the start and the end of the function.

In the main function was a **printf** statement. Statements in C ended in a semi-colon.

```
printf
```

was a standard function that was in the conio.h (console input and output) header file. It displayed and formatted a string on the screen. The string literal *Hello World!* was passed to the printf statement. When the program ran, *Hello world!* flashed on the screen and the program ended. By adding a getch(); function (short for get character), *Hello World!* would remain on the screen until the user pressed a key.

Also included was studying a program that converted Fahrenheit to centigrade.

I was impressed at how the compiler built a single stand-alone executable file. To run the program on a different computer, all you had to do was copy the file to it.

How To Learn Programming

If the program used any data files, they needed to be copied as well. To run an AmigaBasic program, you need to copy over the AmigaBasic interpreter, the source file, and any data files.

Both these sample programs were a lot smaller than AmigaBasic. This is because after a C program was compiled, it would link (add) any libraries that were needed. It would not link **every** file, just the ones that had been included with #INCLUDE directives.

The presenter introduced the KISS principle, which stands for *Keep It Simple, Stupid*. The KISS method is to keep things as simple as possible but not too simple. He advised me to keep it as simple as possible when teaching programming.

Unfortunately, he broke his own rules when he later went into a detailed high-speed dissertation on complex Amiga hardware.

Here are some ideas that can help make a programming task simpler.

You don't need to know all the features of a language in order to write a good program in it.

Minimise the number of data types you use. An ideal situation would be to have only 2 data types: One for strings and one for numbers.

Different number types may result in rounding errors after converting one type to another. This may necessitate casting in different forms.

All my BASIC programs had one source file. This was a nice simple system, but it could get problematic when a program became large. A number of my programs were thousands of lines long.

C programs usually had multiple source files, which had some advantages. This was an example of the programming principle *divide and conquer*. These separate files are called *modules*. The phrase *modular programming* means programming with multiple source files.

There was even a Pascal-like language called Modular-2 at the time. Pascal had replaced BASIC as an introductory language for students.

C was a lot less similar to English than BASIC. It looked both alien and cryptic. However, as I became familiar with it, it appeared quite concise and readable, while BASIC looked verbose by comparison.

In many ways, C is a lot more logical than BASIC. C is still an important language because many later languages are designed to be similar to C, partly so that they are easier to learn.

C keywords were lowercase, while BASIC keywords were in uppercase.

C keywords included:

- int
- char
- short
- long
- unsigned
- for
- while
- do
- break
- continue
- switch
- main
- return
- sizeof
- goto

One of the early ideas of C was to have a relatively small number of keywords that could be easily remembered. Pure C was only about 25 keywords. This would make it easier for programmers to learn and faster to code.

C made much better use of the keyboard than BASIC. C used keyboard characters that were never or rarely used in BASIC, apart from within string literals. For example:

- {} curly brackets
- [] square brackets
- & ampersand
- ^ caret
- % percent
- * asterisk
- ! exclamation mark
- # hash
- ; semi-colon

etc.

Some characters could be used in different contexts. The asterisk could mean about half a dozen different things.

C sometimes replaced words in BASIC with symbols.

For example:

- AND became &&
- OR became ||
- NOT became !
- MOD became %
- FOR, WHILE, SUB etc added {
- NEXT, WEND, END SUB etc became }
- REM became /* */ or // in C++. etc.

A few things in BASIC and C were the same. For example:

- Arithmetic operators + - * /

- \> Greater than.
- \< Less than.
- \>= Greater than or equal to.
- \<= Less than or equal to.
- = Assignment.

An important difference was that in BASIC, = could be used for **assignment**.

```
X = 1
```

and equivalence.

```
IF X = 1 THEN
```

In C, you use = for assignment and == for equivalence. You would write the above as:

```
if(x==1)
etc.
```

Bitwise Operators

BASIC didn't use bitwise operators, so there were no equivalents for:

- & Bitwise And.
- ! Bitwise Not.
- ^ Bitwise XOR.
- | Bitwise Or.
- << Bitwise Left Shift.
- >> Bitwise Right shift.

#define

The convention was that names for constants were wholly in uppercase, though they could include underscores.

For example:

- TOTAL_SCORE
- WHITE
- CURRENT_YEAR

#define WHITE 255 During compilation, wherever WHITE appeared in the source code, it would replaced with 255.

C++ provided an alternative to #define in the form of the keyword **const**. Using **const** had a number of advantages over using #define. One advantage was you could check its value while debugging.

C functions

Functions had a return type, a name, a parameter list and a body. The body needed to include at least one return statement.

For example,

```
int Double(int x)
{
    return x * 2;
}
```

The parameter list is between the brackets, and the body is between the curly brackets.

Scope

Scope in C was different than in BASIC. Variables could be *local*, they only existed within a function. Variables declared outside of functions, usually near the top of a source file, could be used anywhere within that module. Global variables could be used in any file in the program.

A C programmer explained to me in one way scope could be useful. He said imagine if you have a very large program in which you have a number of **for** loops. Some of these loops may call other loops. If you are using **x** as a loop counter for each loop, one loop may inadvertently affect another.

The larger the program, the more useful the scope could be.

C/C++ and JG

I knew JG through a mutual friend in the chess scene. Like my friend, he had bought an Amiga originally for the games. He spent much of the next 3 years on the Amiga, during which time he taught himself programming. Soon, he knew more about programming than many people with computer science degrees.

He told me that learning programming was like learning chess. With learning, you get faster and faster. Your first programming language might take a year to learn. The second language might take 6 months, while the next language might only take a month.

With study and experience, one becomes much more adept at programming. What may have taken you a month as a beginner may only take a day when you are more experienced. Over time, you will get quicker and quicker at writing good code. One of the aims is to make coding as easy as possible.

He mentioned the principle of *delayed gratification*. The basic idea is to get a program working first. Looking good, etc., can come later.

He told me that with C, you could write *tight* code. Tight code is good because it's less to read and less to step through with a debugger. It's also easier to modify. Another programmer once told me much of a programmer's time is spent searching through and reading the code. He mentioned a statistic that, on average, each piece of code is read 10 times, though I don't know the basis for this claim.

A year or two after this, he had switched to the IBM PC. The Commodore Amiga had the best architecture but the worst marketing, and its days were numbered. JG told me the PC was catching up and overtaking every (though most would be more accurate) department.

He showed me some projects he was working on for other people. One was a UFO program, while the other was an astrology program. He told me it was inevitable that I would switch to writing C programs on IBM (these days, people just call them PCs).

The *C* language was the industrial standard in those days. It had taken over dinosaurs such as COBOL and FORTRAN. A relative told me *If it can be written, it can be written in C*. He also said real programmers program in C, a spin on a book titled *Real Men Don't Eat Quiche*.

JG told me how to write a string copy (strcpy) function from scratch. Of course, you don't need to write this, it's one of the standard library functions. He said if I was able to write this, I really understood some aspects of low-level C programming. It's a good exercise that I have given to students in C++ courses to help them understand pointers, indirection, incrementing pointers, etc. He said that with reasonable effort and given my experience in BASIC, I could learn C in 6 months.

Planning

He once said that programming was all in the planning. A well-planned program can be written much faster than a poorly planned one. Within a year or so, he switched to the new C++. In C **x++;** is a shortcut for **x = x + 1;**. (C++ effectively means one better than C). He showed me how classes and objects work. As an exercise, he worked on an impressive project in which he created a Windows-like DOS program.

JG showed me how the Borland C++ compiler built in journal could be used. Compilers usually do not have in built journals, but you can create your own journal. Even a text file could be used. You could add journal entries, including the date, what has been completed, what needs to be done, known bugs, fixed bugs, etc.

Another idea is to create executable files with different version numbers. The first release could be version 1.0. A major revision could add 0.1 to the version number, while a minor revision could add 0.01 to the version number. If there were very major changes to the program, you could change the first number. For example, the first major change could be called version **2.0**.

He once spoke about inviting bugs. Some programming practices which **increase** the likelihood of bugs are:

- Long functions
- Long loops
- Potentially confusing variable names.
- Using the same variable when different variables should be used.
- Unwise use of global variables.
- etc.

Some programming practices which **decrease** the likelihood of bugs are:

- Highly readable code.
- Tight code.
- Only giving variables the scope they need.

Moving to Windows

I followed JG's advice and bought a 386DX IBM-compatible PC. It had a 3.5-inch disk drive plus a 5.25-inch disk drive, which I never used. It had a 120-meg hard drive. I installed Windows 3.1 on it. It was incredibly slow, especially the screen updates. Windows occupied a large part of the hard drive. PC programs occupy a lot of space. I had more programs on my Amiga 20 Meg hard drive than on the PC.

I removed Windows and replaced it with DOS. It ran much better.

A mutual friend of ours had sold his Amiga and had replaced it with a Hercules, which had a black and white monitor and no mouse. What a step down from the Amiga that was.

Dos C++

My first C++ compiler was the then-popular Turbo C++. The *IDE* (Integrated Development Environment) had some very good features. It had a clipboard on which you could copy, cut, paste to and from. This was much better than a clipboard that only stored one block of text, which unfortunately seems to be standard these days.

It had good *debugging* tools. These included:

- You could place *break points* in the code. You could run the program, and it would *break* and enter debug mode when it reached the breakpoint.
- You could add watches. These allowed you to check the values of variables as the program ran.
- You could step into the next statement being executed.
- You could step over function calls.
- And more.

It included a *profiler*, a tool for helping you find out how much time different parts of the program were taking. A profiler is very useful if you are writing a program in which speed is critical. You run a program for a certain amount of time, and the profiler records the frequency of each function. You can see what percentage of time is used for each function. Functions can be inclusive or exclusive of each other. I currently use a profiler called *Very Sleeply* for developing my chess engine. With today's fast computers, many programs are not speed-critical. They do whatever they need to do instantly. The user never has to wait.

Warnings

Compilation created a list of two types of errors. There were normal errors, which was critical. Compilation would fail if there were one or more errors.

There were warnings, which were suggestions that parts of the code were dubious and may result in an error. A programmer I was working with later said something interesting. *Warnings really are errors, its best to fix them.* This is especially true if you if you are being paid for programming.

Typical warnings included things like:

- A local variable is declared but never used.
- A variable is used before it has assigned a value.
- A loop has been created, which has an empty body. In other words, the loop doesn't do anything.

Correcting warnings can be a way of reducing redundant code.

Run time errors

There are certain types of errors that even a C compiler doesn't detect. Run time errors can happen in a C program, though not as frequently as in a BASIC program.

A typical run time error is when a variable is used when it has not yet been assigned a value. For example, if a variable is created as with the statement

```
int x;
```

, its initial value is simply whatever happens to be in that memory location at that time. An integer could have any kind of crazy value in it.

Some languages avoid this by giving variables a default value. Typically, default values might be:

- Zero for numeric types.
- The empty string for strings.
- False for Boolean.
- etc.

Another even more frequent run-time error is an array out-of-bounds error. For example, if an array was declared with

```
int some_array[48];
some_array[57] = 1;
```

will create an error because 57 is greater than 47, the last element in the array.

Even worse, sometimes the error would not be detected and cause memory somewhere else to be overwritten. This could result in a program behaving very strangely. Other variables could take on strange values and so forth.

A negative array index will always result in an out-of-bounds error. For example **some_array[-1]** is going to cause trouble.

A few years later, I learned that a run-time error was called an **exception** and that there were ways of dealing with them.

Strings in C

Strings in C were lower level than in BASIC, which had hid much of the low-level processing.

In memory, one-byte stores one character. A byte was 8 bits, so ASCII codes ranged from 0 to 255 inclusive (28 or 256 in total). A byte fitted a character perfectly.

There is an additional byte to store the end of the string character or *empty string*. The end of the strong character has an ASCII value of zero. Without this, the program will not know where the string ends and will just keep reading the next byte and add it to the string. Note that the empty string character has a different ASCII code than a space.

Hello world stored in a string would look like this in memory (with a pair of square brackets representing one byte):

[H][e][l][l][o][ ][w][o][r][l][d][!][]

In early C, there was no string data type. **char** could be used to represent a single character. For example,

```
char c = 'a';
```

A char variable could also be assigned a number representing an ASCII value. For example,

```
char a = 64;
```

a would have the value of "A" which is the ASCII character with the value of 64.

Strings of more than one character could be created by using an array of type char.

```
char text[256];
```

There were standard library functions that could be used with strings.

For example:

- strcat - Adds to the end of a string.
- strcmp - Compares two strings.
- toascii - Converts a number to an ASCII character.

There were also *macros* that could be used with strings.

For example,

- IsAlpha
- IsNum
- IsUpper

The boundaries between library functions and macros were blurred. A danger of macros is that the macro could expand some text, and then a second macro could expand part of that text again.

Strings Objects in C++

There was a string class that made it possible to use strings at a higher level. For example, you could use + to join two strings.

Decisions

```
if

else

switch
```

C had no ELSEIF keyword like BASIC. Instead, it had the switch statement, which enabled a large number of possible outcomes.

```
switch(x)
{
case 1: do first thing; break;
case 2: do second thing; break;
case 3: do third thing; break;
default:
break;
}
```

The brackets after the **switch** keyword contained the name of a variable. The decision would be based on the value of this variable.

If the value of the variable matches the value after the case keyword, then the following code will be executed.

The **break** keyword was used to jump out of a switch block. Without it, program flow would continue through successive case statements.

The **default** keyword was recommended. The code after default was executed whenever none of the previous case statements were true.

It's possible for a switch statement to have hundreds of case statements.

Loops

There were three types of loops in C.

`for`

which was similar to FOR...NEXT.

`while`

which was similar to WHILE...WEND.

`do...while`

, which was similar to while, except the condition was at the end of the loop instead of the start.

Arrays

Arrays in C were similar to those in BASIC. Instead of using round brackets (), C used square brackets [], which made the code easier to read. It also meant that arrays and function calls would not be confused.

C had the ability to *initialise* the elements of an array.

```
int piece_value[6] =
{
        100, 300, 300, 500, 900, 10000
};
```

Another difference was that C arrays started at zero while BASIC arrays usually started at 1. BASIC had the ability to change this with OPTION BASE, but this was unnecessarily complicated.

The last element in a c array was one less than the size of the array. In BASIC, it was equal to the size. It was important not to get an out-of-bounds array error.

You could have multi-dimensional arrays as in BASIC. This was done by using multiple pairs of square brackets.

For example,

```
int matrix[10][10];
```

creates a 2-dimensional array of 100 elements.

```
int matrix[10][10][10];
```

creates a 3-dimensional array of 1000 elements.

C was less forgiving than BASIC if you referred to an array element that did not exist. Instead of crashing the program, it would often overwrite program memory somewhere, causing bugs that could be difficult to track down.

Structures

Structures were something BASIC didn't have. Unlike arrays, which were a group of variables of the same type, a structure could combine variables of different types.

For example:

```
struct
{
int a;
int b;
char c;
float d;
};
```

Unlike other blocks of code (created with the curly brackets), there was a semi-colon after the closing bracket.

Functions

There were only functions, no subroutines.

Arguments

One or more arguments could be passed to a function. In the function definition, there was a parameter list. Arguments were matched up with parameters.

return

The return statement returned a single value.

The return type was specified in the function declaration.

For example:

```
int GetDouble(int n)
{
int x = 2 * y;
return x;
}
```

returns an integer value. The function could be called by:

```
number = GetDouble(y);
```

void functions

The equivalent of a BASIC subroutine was a **void function**, that one does not return a value. It was possible to use a return statement to leave a void function. This return statement had no return value.

It was possible to return from a void function by

```
return;
```

For example:

```
void some_function(int x)
{
if(x<0) return;
        else
        do something;
```

```
        }
```

Pointers

Pointers were something that BASIC did not have at all.

A pointer is an integer variable that stores a memory address.

You could assign a memory address to a pointer. You could *dereference* the pointer, which would allow you to access the contents of what the pointer was pointing to.

Pointer arithmetic

Pointers can be used with arrays. Let's say a pointer is pointing to an array element. To point to the next element, you could add it to the pointer. The **sizeof** operator could be used to find out how much to *increment* or *decrement* the pointer by.

File handing

As in BASIC, you need to open a file before you can read from it or write to it and close it when finished with it. The file would be physically written to after it was closed.

File handling could cause a run-time error. For example, by trying to open a file that didn't exist.

Debugging in C++

A trick in C++ is to have a block of code commented out with c - style comments.

```
/*
code line 1
code line 2
etc
*/
```

You can uncomment the block by adding a C++ style to the

comments. i.e.

```
//*
code line 1
code lime 2
etc
//*/
```

Nifty eh?

Images

In those days, there was poor support for images. Do you think displaying an image on the screen would be put in the standard library of any programming language. It was not so.

To display an image such as **.bmp, .gif** or **.jpg**, you need dozens maybe hundreds of lines of code. It was possible to copy the code out of books. Fortunately, more programming books started appearing, which included a CD so that you could copy the code from the disk.

Low level

In C, you could do low-level coding that could not be done in BASIC. You could go right down to the bit level.

A bit is the smallest element in computing. It is like an atomic particle that cannot be made any smaller. It's either on or off, with on representing one or true and off representing zero or false.

Assembler

While there were hundreds of functions in the standard C libraries, there were some serious omissions. One of the worst was the lack of mouse support.

One C book I read had **ten pages** of code, which allowed a program to display and read the mouse. Another book showed how to display and read the mouse using about four lines of assembler which could be embedded in the C code. There were no prizes for guessing which way I went.

Unlike the Amiga, which used a hardware sprite for the mouse pointer, the PC used a software sprite.

Using this and some other assembler routines in this book, I had enough information to make some. DOS computer games. For games you could use a screen with dimensions of 320 x 200. The beauty of this was the number of pixels was 64,000. The screen could be represented by a 320 x 200 multi-dimensional array of integers. The 256 colours of this screen were enough to make interesting graphics.

Flight Simulator

One book explained how to create a flight simulator. Flight simulators needed 3-D graphics. To make these possible, a lot of basic trigonometry was needed. Cos, sin, and tan functions were frequently used to rotate an object in 3-D (for example, an aircraft). The book included a complete flight simulator, which allowed the player to *fly* a vintage World War 1 type aircraft.

I once applied for a job with a computer games company. Not only did I get the job, but they offered $10,000 per year extra. Unfortunately, I could only work part-time as I had a young daughter to look after, so I had to let it go.

IBM PC Windows

In those days, while many PCs were running Windows, many were still running DOS. DOS was better for slower computers, while Windows was better for faster computers. JG lamented that OS2 should have been the operating system of the PC.

In those early days of Windows, even a minimalist *Hello World* program took a lot of code, maybe 100 lines. My cousin told me I could write a *Hello World* program in Visual Basic in under 10 minutes, though in C++, it would take a lot longer.

How To Learn Programming

There were numerous programming books containing code examples. In some cases, you need to copy the code. In other cases, it came on a disk. One programmer suggested a method for learning Windows programming. Start with some source code written by someone else. Make some small changes, run the program and see the results.

I developed a Windows game, which I hoped to release commercially. It involved wizards battling by casting spells at each other. I had a good collection of sound samples recorded by a sound engineer, a graphics artist and a willing distributor.

At one point during development, it was discovered that after a long session, the program would crash Windows. The cause was difficult to track down. It turned out it was a *memory leak*, which was very easy to create at that time. It was insidious. There were no warnings or error messages. It couldn't be found by ordinary debugging.

At a few points in the program, I used a library function called DeleteDC instead of ReleaseDC (or perhaps the other way around). Every time this happened, a small amount of RAM was lost to the operating system. Slowly, Windows would run out of RAM and crash.

Programmers were usually protected from memory leaks in BASIC. In C, though, it was an issue. Some programs would assign a pointer to a block of memory. The program would end without releasing the memory and no other program, including the operating system, until the computer was rebooted.

The Turbo C++ and its successor, Borland C++, were easier to use than Visual C++. Borland introduced colour coding of the source code. Initially, it looked gimmicky, but it turned out to be quite useful. Comments, variables, keywords, string values, etc., were all in different colours. It made the code easy to read.

Hungarian Notation

One book I read recommended using *Hungarian notation*. The idea of this was variable names could have a prefix that indicated what variable type they were.

Something similar happened automatically to some extent in BASIC. String variables ended in a dollar sign. For example, A$ could be the name of a string variable.

In C, you could prefix all your char variables with a lowercase c, floats could be prefixed with an f, doubles with a d, etc.

Web Pages

In the early 90s, I joined the net around the same time that *Sausage Hot Dog* made 50,000,000 dollars for its author. This HTML editor was very ordinary by later standards, but he got in first.

I took over a website called the Victorian Chess Pages. For a number of years, it was getting 2,000 hits per week.

The host Vicnet, which was part of the State Library, allowed a *generous* 2 A4 pages of space for the website. I guess that is about two screen fulls. To update the website, one had to copy the HTML file to a floppy disk and post it to Vicnet by snail mail.

FTP

A mechanism was needed to upload files to your website. **File Transfer Protocol** was one way. I used a free program called WS_FTP in the early days. You could save your passwords, default directories etc. The program displayed two directories:

- One on the local machine (your computer).
- One on the host machine (the server).

You could simply select files and click on upload. A great sound effect was played when there was a successful upload. Rarely you might wish to download your files from the server. I later switched to another program called FileZilla.

HTML

I did learn the basics of HTML. Including:

- Formatting text
- Hyperlinks
- Lists
- Tables

- Images
- CGI scripts
- Forms
- etc.

Some HTML features were more common in those days. The **blink** tag, which created flashing text and frames have largely vanished. Given how many people they annoyed, it's little wonder why. Unfortunately, the frequency of things moving around on a web page while you are trying to read it seems to be on the rise.

HTML was not a complete programming language. It did not have decisions, loops, function calls, etc. An HTML page basically gives instructions to the browser on how to render the page. The instructions are mostly followed in order.

The main exception is a *hyperlink*, which functioned a bit like a **goto** in a general programming language.

With a hyperlink *Program flow* could go:

- Somewhere else on the same page.
- A different page on the same website.
- To a different website entirely.
- To a file on the same page. Clicking on this link would cause the file to start downloading. For example, you could upload a **.zip** file to your page and create a link to it.

  A file would be opened by the appropriate program. For example, a **.pdf** file would be opened by Abode Acrobat.

CGI scripts were not as popular as they used to be. They were used for features such as Visitor Counters on web pages.

The general programming language JavaScript could be added to a web page to make it more interactive.

UNIX C

I spent a year maintaining C code in a Unix environment for a company that developed insurance software. The slow, non-graphical interface seemed very archaic to me. The good news for me was that UNIX was quite similar to AmigaDos, the operating system of the old Amiga.

There were a few neat features, though. One was an option that automatically indented the code, which is not trivial to program for C source code.

A program would take minutes to compile.

One of the existing programs had the largest loop I had ever seen spanning several **thousand** lines of code. This is not usual practice normally a large amount of code within a loop would be placed in functions.

One programmer there once stated that he didn't use comments, he wrote self-documenting code. There is some sense to this. Good choice of user-defined names and other programming practices and reduce the need for comments.

The company went under as a result of not changing with the times.

SQL

One thing that I was introduced to in this job was the SQL language. It stood for structured query language and was used in conjunction with databases. I was told it was pronounced *sequel* It's important to note that SQL is not a programming language.

The basics of SQL were pretty easy to learn. However, there were finer points of SQL that would take much longer to master.

FM Bill Jordan

The most frequently used command was **SELECT**. This allowed the user to create a selection of records that matched the specified criteria.

Introduction to Programming at the CAE

While working at the Insurance software company, I received a phone call from the CAE (Council of Adult Education). A year earlier, I proposed Computer Games programming as a possible new course. They were not interested in that course at the time but were interested in a replacement tutor for their *Introduction to Programming* course. Soon, I was presenting the Qbasic *Hello World* program.

```
?"A"Hello World
```

After pressing Enter, this would expand to

```
PRINT "Hello World"A"
```

Pressing F5 would run the program. How easy was that?

The Qbasic manual provided exercises in which students copied code and ran the programs. They didn't need to write any original code. I didn't think that would be enough to challenge the students, but I didn't anticipate their typos, which would create errors in their programs. They would then have to hunt down the cause of the errors.

How do people learn? It has been said that people retain relatively little information if they have only heard it. If they have seen it and are able to do it, then the retention rate will be 90%.

There was a glitch in my first tutorial. The connection between the computer I was using and the overhead projector wasn't working, so without my knowledge, it wasn't showing on the screen. From where I was, I couldn't see it, and the students didn't say anything. After I discovered it, it never happened again.

FM Bill Jordan

I was to spend the next 10 years being an IT tutor at the CAE, tutoring thousands of students in hundreds of courses. I ran a dozen or so different courses.

Courses included:

- Introduction to programming.
- Introduction to VB.
- Intermediate VB.
- Advanced VB.
- Design your own web pages.
- Introduction to HTML
- HTML part 2.
- Introduction to Outlook.
- Java
- C++
- VBA
- Excel
- XML
- DOS

There were students from a variety of different organisations. There were people from MYOB (Mind Your Own Business), which was a software package for small businesses. There were members of the police force who wanted to design forms in VB. There were people from Lonely Planet, a company that produces travel guides. There were people from the ANZ bank. There were people from the Bureau of Meteorology. There was someone from the Department of Defence. He said that they used DOS, which they considered more reliable than Windows. There was my old Amiga student.

Classes were typically 3 hours. In classes, I would usually give a short lecture, say 15-30 minutes. Then, the students would do exercises and call out when they got stuck, and I would do my best to help them. If a question stumped a lot of students, I would go through it so that the whole class could see it on the overhead screen.

How To Learn Programming

Classes ranged from 3 to 15 students. Some classes were in the evenings, some during the day, while others were on Saturdays, and a few were even on Sundays. Classes were mostly about four sessions. Each student had a desktop computer. When I started, all the students' computers were facing the front. This was good for the students as they could see their screen and use their computer while being able to see the trainer, whiteboard and overhead projector. One day, I came into a class and found that the room had been completely changed. All the students' computers were facing the walls. This was good for the tutors because they could easily see all the screens. The downside was that students were forever turning around to alternate between looking at the front and looking at their own screen.

One student said it was better learning programming in a class than on your own. Being in a class stops you from falling asleep. It turned out her husband's father was one of the directors of General Motors.

Training the Trainer

At one stage, I did a one-day training course for trainers. The trainer described himself as a *touchy-feely* sort of guy. The participants were involved in a few ice-breaking exercises. One was to form small groups. Each person in a group would adjust something about their appearance without the others seeing them. They then had to guess what was different about their appearance. We were told not to do what one woman once did for this exercise, which was to remove all her clothes.

The main thing I remember from that course was that there is a tendency for trainers to pour a lot of knowledge into the students. He said it was not just about content. Students needed to be able to absorb information at their own rate. It was also about giving them a good experience.

An important idea was for the trainer to share his **passion** with the students.

Another idea was to give extra time to the weaker students rather than the better students. The more experienced students were more likely to be committed, while the less experienced were more likely to get discouraged and drop out.

Making Programming Fun

Programming is potentially frustrating. If you need instant gratification or get upset when reaching a minor obstacle, then you probably won't enjoy programming. If you don't enjoy it, then you will probably stop doing it.

It has been said that *Stupidity is doing the same thing over again and again and expecting a different result.*

One thing that can be not enjoyable can be getting *stuck* on something. In these cases, it may be good to change your approach.

A good approach is not to get upset when your code doesn't behave as it is meant to. You need to be flexible. Often, the cause of a bug is not what you think it is. You sometimes need a different approach. Every bug can be seen as a learning experience.

What is a program?

It is a series of instructions that a computer follows.

I told students that all programs have three parts to them:

- Input
- Processing
- Output

Input

Input could come from a variety of sources. It could come from the keyboard, the mouse, a microphone or from a variety of gaming devices such as a joystick. As well as coming from the user, input could come from a file.

Processing

Programs process the input in some way.

Output

Output could be directed to a variety of locations. It could go to a screen, a file, a printer, the Internet, the speakers, etc. It could even go to an input device. For example, a program could move the mouse to a certain location.

The simplest possible computer that has these three components is a light switch:

- The switch is the input.
- The processing is the connection between the switch and the light.
- The light is the output. It's either on or off.

A light switch is also similar to the smallest unit on a computer, the **bit**. A bit stores either **1** or **0**. The zero sometimes represents **false** while the 1 represents **true**.

Visual Basic

Microsoft
Visual Basic 6.0

The same week, I started the course using Qbasic, a visual basic course. I had used Visual Basic for DOS but had done little with VB for Windows. One student remarked that VB sounded like a brand of beer, which it did (Victoria Bitter).

In many ways, VB was similar or identical to older versions of BASIC, such as AmigaBasic or QuickBasic. For example, arrays were similar. Once, I demonstrated how to create an array in VB. I wrote on the whiteboard

```
Dim students
```

One student spontaneously remarked. *Dim students, yes, that's us.* The **Dim** is short for *dimension* and is the traditional BASIC command for creating arrays.

VB had some great features which made it possible to code quickly. Like older versions of BASIC, it was case insensitive. Unlike older versions of BASIC, which turned entire words uppercase, VB used title-case or proper-case, in which only the first letter in a word is uppercase. This was more convenient than joining words together with underscores, as in C programs.

How To Learn Programming

For example,

```
Dim ProperCase as String
```

In VB, almost everything could be typed in lowercase. Any word VB could recognise would be converted to title-case.

When user-defined words, such as variable names, function names, etc, were first used, they could be written using upper and lowercase letters.

Typing a string constant was another situation in which it might be necessary to type both upper and lowercase letters. For example, if you typed "Hello World!"A", you would need to manually type upper and lowercase letters. For the most part, though, you could type everything in lowercase, and you completed the line by pressing Enter; the editor would automatically change the case when needed.

The editor would also insert spaces, for the most part. For example, if you typed the closing part of an If statement:

```
endif
```

It would expand to:

```
End If
```

VB used a great combination of case insensitivity and upper and lower case letters. VB was quicker to type than C++ or Java. In fact, case-sensitive language can cause bugs.

For example, imagine if there are variables

```
Total_Score and Total_score
```

within the same scope. Confusing these could cause obscure logic bugs.

Another good feature of VB was *intellisense*. If you started typing something VB recognised, it would *pop up* your possible choices or sometimes complete the word for you. If you typed some text and pressed space or a full stop, it would display choices.

A downside of a poorly designed **intellisense** is that it could pop up irrelevant choices.

Debugging

VB had a great debugger. You had the usual debugging tools:

- Step Over
- Step Into
- Breakpoints
- Watches etc.

It had the best of both the interpreted and compiled world. Interpreted languages are easier to debug because some errors can be fixed **while** the program is running. When you wanted to release it you could compile it.

One day, I was talking about bugs and mentioned the following:

Murphy's law says that whatever can go wrong will go wrong and at the worst possible time.

One student commented. *Murphy's law was invented for programmers.*

The trend over the years was for BASIC to become more and more like C. VB had the Select Case statement, which was similar to the C switch statement. The main difference was that there was no break keyword. It was implicit.

Functions could have optional arguments. For example, the same function might be called by passing one, two or three arguments. Optional arguments could reduce the number of needed functions.

VB had *types*, which were similar to structures in C and classes as in C++.

There were two sides to VB. There was the program code, which was somewhat hidden away. There were the objects, which included *forms* and *controls*.

Objects

Like C++ and other object-oriented programs (OOP), VB uses objects. Objects had properties, methods and events.

Properties

A property is an **attribute** of an object.

For example, a Label had a **text** property.

Methods

A method is something an object **does**.

For example, a TextBox had a **SetFocus** method.

Events

An event is something that happens to an object **does**. Not all objects had events.

For example, a Button had a **click** event.

Forms

VB programs typically had one or more *forms*, though it was conceivable that you might have a VB program without them. A form is a window. It had properties such as:

- A title.
- Width and height.
- Position of the top left corner.

- etc.

Controls

Controls were objects represented by small icons, which you could place on a form. In *Design mode*, creating your form and controls was a bit like using a paint program. There were many types of controls.

Controls included:

- Buttons for clicking on.
- Labels for displaying text.
- Text boxes for users to enter text into.
- Image controls for displaying images.
- And many more.

Event Driven Programming

Windows programming involved a style a program that didn't happen in DOS or UNIX environments. Normally, a program starts at the start and flows down from statement to statement.

In a Windows program, everything is loaded. Usually, the initial form, and then the program waits for the user to do something.

The pseudo-code of the main program logic could be like this:

```
Do
If the user does something, then
response
end if
Loop
```

What is an event?

Events are mostly done by the user. They include:

- Mouse events (Clicking, double-clicking, moving the mouse etc.)

- Keyboard events (keypress etc.)
- Focus events

Other events included:

- Load (loading something into memory).

VB Hello World program

You could create a VB Hello World program by:

- Starting a new project.
- Add a button to the default Form.
- Double click on the button to generate the *stub* for the default event procedure.
- The cursor will be in the middle of the procedure. Type **messagebox..** When you type the full stop, IntelliSense will suggest the word **show**. Select that, then type **("Hello World!**and press enter. The closing quotations and brackets will be added.
- Run the program.

```
Public Class Form1
    Private Sub Button1_Click(ByVal sender As
System.Object, ByVal e As System.EventArgs) Handles
Button1.Click
        MessageBox.Show("Hello world")
    End Sub
End Class
```

Note that most of the code has been generated.

I once wrote a VB quiz program with 5000 questions, many of them on properties, methods and events. Other VB programs I wrote for my own amusement included:

- A *front-end* for a C++ compiler. There was a command-line C++ compiler I was using. To make life easier, I spent a few days putting together a VB program that created a nice compiler interface. It used a *Shell* command to call the compiler from the VB program.

- A program for solving Sudoku puzzles.
- A program for creating old-style text adventures. These days, they call text adventures *Interactive Fiction*.
- I experimented with using VB for creating animation but found it much too slow. It was much better suited to applications than games.

VBA

I also taught Visual Basic for Applications, i.e. for Microsoft Office programs, mostly for Excel. With VBA, you could record a macro, which is essentially creating a VBA program by recording your actions.

You could also create a program from scratch. VBA was great for automating repetitive tasks. If you were doing a lot of repetition on a spreadsheet, it was time to start looking at writing a VBA program.

VBA courses were held during the day, while most other courses were held during the evening. During day courses, we would have a class lunch at the nearby *Cafe Brassiere*. It was a good bonding experience, which helped to make classes more enjoyable. One evening, two students shouted at the whole class for a meal.

I worked for several months for the Bureau of Meteorology using VBA with Excel spreadsheets, which contained information about thousands of items, mostly radar parts.

Flight Planner

I worked for a little over a year developing flight planning software for light aircraft pilots and a financial forecasting program. The software was written in VB.

Pascal

I read a book on the Pascal language, which had replaced BASIC as an introductory programming language for computer science students. Pascal was designed to be more structured than BASIC, and it was designed to teach students good programming habits. A few years I converted a poorly written Pascal program into VB for a company that ran sporting events.

HTML

In HTML classes, I described the Internet as a giant book with millions of pages. New pages were continually being added while a smaller number were continually being removed.

In one HTML class, a student surprised everyone by producing a baby possum from her jacket pocket.

After a basic introduction, students were encouraged to develop their own websites.

Java

Java was one of a number of programming languages I introduced at the CAE. The C language evolved over a number of years and eventually transformed into C++. Java, in contrast, was designed. The intention was to create a language that avoided some of the problems with C/C++.

A major source of bugs in C/C++ was the erroneous use of pointers. A friend of mine wiped his hard drive by overwriting it, starting at address zero. Pointers pointing at the wrong thing could cause mayhem. In Java, instead of using pointers, you have references. References always have to be pointing at something real. There were approximately 40 differences between Java and C/C++.

Java was designed to be multi-platform and also run on the net in the form of applets.

There was a lot of great software written in Java. However, from a coding point of view, it has weaknesses that C/C++ doesn't have and some weaknesses it didn't need to have.

It has the *enary* **ternary** operator. This was an unnecessary complication and makes the code harder to read. Apparently, it was hotly debated whether it should be added to Java or not. I would have voted **no**.

Another one is *multiple inheritance*, which is not needed (C++ doesn't have it) and has the potential to cause great confusion, especially with programmers not experienced with it.

It is more verbose than necessary.

Unicode

Java had support for Unicode was like a greatly extended ASCII character set. Unicode included characters in different languages and many other symbols.

C++ and One Computer

An Indian student mentioned that the school in his village had only one computer. Students would write their programs on paper. The teacher would type their code on the computer and test the programs. They were effectively writing their programs blind. This had some advantages to normal ways of learning as well as disadvantages.

C++ and Dark Basic

When I was short-listed to one for a role tutoring computer game programmers, I wrote a couple of rough 3D games using the Dark Basic library. In one, I created a character that ran around a hilly country, while in the other, I created a simple flight simulator. Dark Basic is one of a number of packages around designed to make game programming easier. It was coding in C++, but using the libraries was like coding games in Amos Basic, which is a higher level language than C++.

JavaScript

JavaScript, despite its name, is not especially like Java. It's more like a version of Basic using C syntax. It has variables, loops, functions and so forth. It fits in well with HTML to make a web page dynamic.

It can be used to write simple online 2-D educational programs and games. I have written a chess playing program in JavaScript.

Learning a New Language

Programmers frequently need to learn a new language. What are some ways that could make learning quicker and more effective? Reading about programming is not enough. You need to get your hands dirty.

One way to start is to write a minimalist **Hello world** type program. All you need to do is display the phrase *Hello world!* on the screen.

Learn how to do some common tasks in the new programming languages

Examples may include:

- Display text on the screen.
- Display an image on the screen.
- Get keyboard input from the user.
- Get mouse input from the user.
- Read and write to a file.
- Learn how to use the debugger.

Don't take anything for granted. You don't know for certain something works until you have successfully tested it. Some things will be easy in some languages while being difficult in others.

Comparisons

Most languages have a lot in common with other languages.

One way to learn a new language is to compare it with a known one. You could compare it feature by feature and make notes about similarities and differences. You can compare the features of the new language with those of one you know well.

Examples of features may include:

- Comments.
- Rules for user-defined names.
- Type of variables.
- Constants.
- Loops with a known number of iterations.
- Loops with an unknown number of iterations.
- Decisions.
- Functions
- Passing arguments.
- Optional arguments.
- Returning a value.
- String manipulation.
- File handling.

A feature may be identical.

A feature may be functionally identical but with a slight difference For example, a word may be spelled slightly differently.

A feature may be quite different. These are the ones you will likely need to spend the most time on.

The feature may be absent in one of the languages.

Converting a program

To help familiarise myself with Java, I ported a largish (10,000+ lines) C++ program to Java. I learned much about the similarities and differences between the two programs. Much of the code didn't need to be changed.

The first step was to develop the Java program to a point where all the syntax errors were removed. The next step was to remove the more subtle errors. In a serious program, thorough testing would need to be done for such a large conversion.

Writing a quiz

Writing a quiz program can be a good exercise. It can include user input, output on the screen, file handling (questions and answers can be in an external file), etc. You can choose what questions you want. When I was learning C, I wrote a quiz on C to help me develop familiarity with its strange-looking syntax.

Doing quizzes written by others could also be very useful:)

Teaching Others

Another possible way to learn is by teaching a friend or a relative.

The Monster Programming Language

An idea I had is to create a teaching language that encompasses many languages. It could be used as a matrix of features.

My Ideal language

My ideal language would be easy to code, read and debug. It would produce fast, efficient code. It would be able to do anything the hardware was capable of doing. To make it easy to code, it would be case insensitive, similar to VB. It would use **intellisense** but not pop up irrelevant options.

The syntax would be similar to C syntax.

It would have a small set of keywords with no redundant keywords. There would be no obsolete keywords present to maintain *backward compatibility*. Keywords would all be in lowercase.

Variables

Variables would have default values like Java. The compiler would be intelligent enough to ???

Arrays

Arrays would use [] as in C. This makes the code easier to read.

Strings

Strings could be basic like. They could have a $ at the end to indicate that they are a string. Concatenation is common enough that + for strings could be part of the language.

I would not have operator overloading. In the early days of C++, a lot of misuse of operator overloading caused mayhem.

Functions and classes could be reused easily. You could plug in classes without any issues.

Debugging would have plenty of features, including:

- Ability to add/remove/find breakpoints.
- Ability to break when a condition happens.
- Ability to watch values of variables.
- Ability to edit source easily while in debug mode.
- etc.

Backward compatibility

Newer versions of programming languages sometimes continue outdated features for no reason but to make the current version backwardly compatible with earlier versions. My Ideal language would not do this.

Editor

The editor would have plenty of features that would make it easier to code quickly and well.

- Automatic indentation.
- Color coding.
- intellisense.
- etc.

Where to go to from here?

It is easy for me to make small changes and update this book. If you have any constructive suggestions, you can email me at **swneerava@gmail.com**. Positive reviews are welcome.

About the Author

Bill Jordan is a self-taught programmer who created a large number of programs for the Public Domain. He has worked as a programmer for several companies and on various programs for others. He was an IT trainer for 10 years, tutoring adults. He is also a national senior chess champion and has a number of chess books available on Amazon.

www.ingramcontent.com/pod-product-compliance
Lightning Source LLC
LaVergne TN
LVHW051708050326
832903LV00032B/4082